THE GREAT BRITISH NEIGHBOUR DISPUTE

Alistair Ford

Grosvenor House
Publishing Limited

This book is published by
Grosvenor House Publishing Ltd
Link House
140 The Broadway, Tolworth, Surrey, KT6 7HT.
www.grosvenorhousepublishing.co.uk

A CIP record for this book
is available from the British Library

ISBN 978-1-83975-436-4

The Anticipation

The moment you receive the keys to your new home is unforgettable.

This is the time you can relax, knowing that all of the searching, paperwork and logistics is over.

You are ready to plan your new life.

You eagerly have the home improvement plans in draft.

The house is there to transform to your exacting specification.

Yet, there is the great unknown.

Your neighbours.

Who are they?

What is their background?

And most importantly of all... how are they going to relate to you.

If you are lucky enough to have excellent neighbours and have no issues whatsoever, you can place this book back on your retailer's shelf and progress over to the Nigella Lawson cookery books.

However, if you are unlucky enough to have potential neighbour issues, this book profiles the personalities you are likely to meet. With my careful research, this is the home dwellers first point of reference.

But first we need to consider how to avoid having neighbours in the first place.

The Home

In an ideal world, to avoid having neighbours, your home would be a country mansion. The only neighbours you would have to worry about would be the deer and pheasants which would wander through your country estate.

There is also the small matter of buying the property in the first place, you would have been successful in setting up a multi-million pound business, composed a series of hit records, or be able to write and shift millions of copies of books... hopefully – for me – like the one you are now reading.

There is, of course, the maintenance of the grounds, and your hover mower may take a full week to cut the grass. You will have to have deep pockets to maintain the fabric of the house and employ an army of staff just to keep the maintenance ongoing.

You may need to open up the house and grounds to the public to assist with costs, which brings about the bureaucracy of insurance, health and safety, co-ordination of events, all which takes time and energy.

Then there is the rather small matter of the threat of HS2 or a bypass being cut through the grounds, or a fracking site set up nearby.

You can also never read *The Guardian* with a clear conscience without reference being made to your wealth and the benefits of a Land Value tax.

But the major benefit would be no neighbours... not unless you wish to declare feudal war with the neighbouring estate.

However, most of us do not have the means to be able to purchase such a property, so the next best thing needs to be considered.

At the other end of the spectrum, there is the option to live in a soon-to-be-redeveloped derelict estate.

With residents having departed, there is an abundance of available properties. Ranging from studio apartments to semi-detached houses, you are spoilt for choice.

There is the small issue of the property lacking windows or amenities, however, if you use your imagination, the refuse laden gardens can be transformed into an idyllic setting.

Like your country house counterpart, you need not worry about parking either. As all of the neighbouring houses are sheeted up, it means there will be an abundance of parking spaces. The additional benefit is the parking will only need to be used for one night because your car will no longer be there in the morning. This may be an issue if your car is on a monthly PCP deal, however, if your preferred form of transport is either free through resuscitating an abandoned car, or stolen, this need not be a concern.

Still, if you are not in the happy position of being able to reside in either property, there is a need to compromise. You will therefore have to live next door to neighbours. And here we start the tour of the types of neighbours you could be lucky to meet...

Case Study 1 – The Suburban Aspirational Go-Getter

Case Study 2 – The Party Animal

Case Study 3 – The Eager Listener

Case Study 4 – The Downturner

Case Study 5 – The Grudge

Case Study 6 – The Territorial

Case Study 7 – The Absentee

Case Study 8 – The Fortress

Case Study 9 – Bringing Your Work Home

Case Study 10 – Walkies

Case Study 11 – Car Status Arms Race

Case Study 12 – The Random Car

Case Study 13 – The Inquisitor

Case Study 14 – The Mad Driver

Case Study 15 – The Social Leader

Case Study 16 – The Objector

Case Study 17 – The Watcher

Case Study 18 – The Challenger

Case Study 19 – The Liberty Taker

Case Study 20 – Home Deliveries

Case Study 21 – The Security Junkie

Case Study 1 – The Suburban Aspirational Go-Getter

Starting our profiles with a positive note, upon first impressions, the omens are good. The house is neat, the driveway is clear, and they add value to your home. What is not to like?

There is no doubt the Suburban Aspirational Go-Getter is on their way up.

The extension of ego and style matches the size of the housing development.

In its strictest sense, the Suburban Aspirational Go-Getter really ought to live in a large country mansion with a long gravel drive and extensive grounds.

The reality is they live in the same standard specification house which the rest of the residents live in. The only difference is they like to magnify their success in the ever so micro world they live in.

Take, for example, education. Most of us went to school and left with a selection of exam results. Some results were good, others less so. Some of us did very well and left with a string of As.

The Suburban Aspirational Go-Getter will let you know they went to a good school and had an exceptionally good education. They will also say they did very well in their exams, even if the Grade D results met a grim ending with the office shredder. Worse, they will be the ones who will constantly talk up their children's results, pressurising the poor souls to keep up. On results day, they will announce that their offspring achieved grade As and a First-Class honours degree. Naturally, their children will have already become a Captain of Industry at the age of 24. The reality may be a dead-end job, unsorting household waste at the incinerator 200 miles down the road.

The Suburban Aspirational Go-Getter uses language to uprate everything they have bought and achieved, and never admit to anything going wrong. Their job is always going really well, and they have a title such as Director or Senior Executive. It goes without saying that they claim to go on holiday to somewhere which sounds expensive and which you have never heard of.

They assure you their mid-market saloon car rides like a Rolls Royce, particularly when your wheels would be in the target group for scrappage. Worse still, they invite you for a ride around the estate in their car to demonstrate how good it is, and you fail to make an excuse why you must get away.

The Suburban Aspirational Go-Getter never has a downfall and nothing apparently ever goes wrong in their lives. You know full well in the social pecking order of the street, the Suburban Aspirational Go-Getter is top of the tree.

Yet one of the mysteries which remains unsolved is, if the Suburban Aspirational Go-Getter is doing that good, why are they still living in the same house, have never updated it, have the same bathroom suite the developer installed, and the new carpet is the same pattern laid back in 1984.

LOUD
PARTY
LAGER
VOLUME
LOUD
V.LOUD
EARTH SHUDDER

Case Study 2 – The Party Animal

Council tax records will show there is one resident at this address. In fact, the number is closer to six. Like a fading pop group, the line-up does change. But let us not prompt a tax investigation. We will focus on the official resident.

The Party Animal has excellent interpersonal skills and is exceptionally reliable.

These qualities are ideal in the workplace as they are vital to improvement and business productivity.

However, the definition is rather different in a residential setting as this means there is going to be a social gathering every Friday and Saturday night.

If the Party Animal has truly exceptional interpersonal skills, this would mean they have their social circle around from Monday until Thursday as well.

In this age of loneliness, you need never feel alone.

The party usually gets going at 6.00pm, then extends through until 4.00am in the morning. If you work nights, then you do have the benefit of a quiet day to rest up.

The Party Animal also provides excellent security for your property in the event there is a garden function.

The music tastes are consistent and usually involve a constant electronic base and beat. And whilst your choice of music compilation may last one hour, their value for money is streets ahead with a full 12 hours' worth of beats.

As the Party Animal has a diverse range of guests, the evening can cumulate in a spot of DIY at 3.00am in the morning, whereby they will be doing something useful like building a fitted wardrobe or demolishing the fireplace.

At the functions, the beverages are usually served in recycled packages which – unfortunately – do not always make it to the green bin. You do at least acquire a full and comprehensive knowledge of value mass produced beer and lager brands, with bottles of cider thrown in.

The Party Animal and guests may be in receipt of medication and receive a home delivery service. Unfortunately, invoices can be paid late, and the providers may send around their debt collection officers who are highly effective but have occasional issues with their use of Satnav.

There is no doubt that the Party Animal has the drive and determination, as they can survive on 2 hours sleep every night and still carry out a day's work.

And because they are so social, you just cannot bring yourself to complain, so you remain shattered and are enrolled on performance improvement measures because you fell asleep on the desk at work.

Case Study 3 – The Eager Listener

After living with the Party Animal, it does come something as a culture shock when there is a firm knock at the door and you are asked to keep the noise down.

Meet the Eager Listener.

Your life has already been quiet. Your TV and stereo are set to a low volume. There has been no DIY taking place. Surely, what could the issue be?

The Eager Listener has super sensitive hearing which should be deployed at Fylingdales or Menwith Hill Early Warning Listening Stations. If enemy states could genetically engineer their spies, the Eager Listener would be the result.

The big issue is that your TV is too loud. You are taken aback as once you leave the lounge; you cannot it hear it in the next living space, let alone the kitchen. You apologise and turn the volume down even further.

Then you receive a further knock at the door. The Eager Listener is furious that you are inconsiderate, and they can hear your TV through the wall. And your central heating clanks water through the pipes. This is unheard of, so you call the plumber around and they agree it is not an issue. Which is just as well as the replacement system will be a four-figure sum.

Then the letter from the Environmental Health department at the local council drops through your letterbox. You are in breach of Noise Nuisance legislation and you will be served a notice if this continues. The culprit is not only your TV, but your central heating pipes, and your barking dog, which you do not own or reside with. And apparently, you can be heard talking through the walls too. This sets you off into a state of paranoia as you frantically recall conversations you may have possibly had which you really did not want to make. You study your bank and credit card statements just to make sure the Eager Listener has not been internet shopping at your expense.

Of course, that would not happen. The Eager Listener is squeaky clean and goes to Church every Sunday. Which is why they are believed, and you are not.

Guilty as charged.

BILL
$1000
DIVORCE
BILL
$12500
DEBT
LAST
CHANCE
RED
REMINDER

Case Study 4 – The Downturner

Some people can enter a room and the whole room lights up.

Some people can enter a room and the lights turn a dim shade of off yellow. Not a blackout, but a low dim light which slowly affects and corrodes your previously good mood.

The Downturner often has a sorry tale to tell. Their spouse has left them after having an affair. They have lost their job. Their former house has either been repossessed or handed to their spouse post-divorce. The divorce lawyer was not particularly competent and racked up a £15k bill so they could have 20% of the family home. In addition, it was one of those Family Law firms which dresses up the most wretched and dredged out periods of your life presented in the same positive light as a day out to a Family Theme Park.

When the Downturner moves into their new home, it is newly presented, eagerly awaiting its new occupier. Then the rot sets in. Plant pots contain dead plants. A week's worth of washing up mounts up at the kitchen window. Refuse is hoarded in the kitchen to save having to use another bin liner for cost and not because they have become an environmentalist. Light bulbs are not replaced. Dead flies appear at the window. The grass grows ever longer.

If the Downturner is harmless enough, they remain a quiet enough neighbour. The car is usually parked in the drive out of the way. They don't pick arguments. An untidy lawn is much better than some of the other characters profiled in this book. If you are happy with a quiet life, you can do no worse and hope their life remains in the doldrums so that the next decade can pass without incident.

The one to avoid is the Downturner who has a dark past. And worse can morph into the Grudge.

And this is one we will profile next.

STORAGE BOX.
TAKEAWAY

YUK!
PONG!

Case Study 5 – The Grudge

There is a rule where even if you are the nicest person in the world, not everyone will like you.

And so, we introduce the Grudge.

The Grudge, for whatever reason, takes an instant dislike to you. They may not like your cheerful demeanour. Or it may be the car you drive. Or the new driveway you have just laid. Perhaps your greenhouse isn't quite to their taste.

Whatever it is, the Grudge has decided that you are something they absolutely detest, and it is in their DNA to let you know indirectly.

The first thing you may notice is they will ignore you when you say "Hello".

Or they may chat to one of their equally weird social circle and point towards you or your property.

The Grudge works in mysterious ways. Dog dirt suddenly appears next to the driver's door where you are parked. Or your wiper blades are pulled up for no apparent reason with an unrepeatable message daubed in the dirt on your rear tailgate. Fence posts suddenly uproot themselves. You find yourself on the mailing list of a retail chain usually found on motorways, with a name resembling a trendy wine bar. Human excrement appears on your rear flagged patio despite you having invested in security lighting.

To continue the similar theme to a fine art, the Grudge can even have the knack of defecating in the middle of a busy roundabout and not being noticed.

There is a conspiracy theory that the Grudge works for the security devices industry. You start finding yourself interested in websites for CCTV, gates and fences, progressing to your home looking like Unit 15, Bellathorpe Industrial Estate.

Whatever happens, the Grudge will never quite go away and will intermittently make their presence felt.

If you are lucky, the Grudge moves on. The circumstances are never known. It could be a divorce, a job promotion involving relocation, a new relationship after advertising their dazzling personality on an online dating website, or just being sent to prison.

Nature has a way of filling a vacuum, so we say goodbye to the Grudge and welcome in...

Case Study 6 – The Territorial

When a property is purchased, the ownership often comprises of the house, the garden, parking and access rights.

The footpath, road and street furniture are often the property of the local council.

So far so good?

Technically, this should be where the matter ends, however, there are some residents within the midst who are still in a Cold War style mentality. They often think their territory needs to be expanded or extend their sphere of influence.

Take for example parking facilities.

There is a natural order to parking. The usual idea is for your car to be parked on your own drive or outside your own home.

However, the Territorial has other ideas and thinks their four cars should be parked outside their own drive and on the street. And they will be parked on the street outside their house and their neighbours.

Usually the vehicle is parked 2cm away from your car, so you feel obliged to move it away. You watch the Territorial drive away signalling in the wrong direction whilst still on their phone, threatening to scrape your car in the process.

The favour does not tend to be returned. In the event, a car is parked outside the Territorial's house, the owner then receives a note asking for the vehicle to be moved. It is written in the same tone as if the author has been sacked, the house has been repossessed and the partner has decided to run off with the betting shop owner.

These incidents do occasionally apply opportunities for the car scratch repair industry.

Signs start appearing on public roads threatening to tow away vehicles. And there are of course the inevitable Residents Only signs, preceded by the blue P symbol. The downside is they read as "Presidents Only", leading to the local wind up merchant posting pictures of Clinton, Putin and Trump on their front wall.

Then there is the issue of street furniture. The Territorial takes ownership as to where lamp posts are sited and insists that the council places it outside an alternative property to theirs. This results in a game of cat and mouse as neighbours bid for the lamp post to be moved around the street with the end result being intended for all eight lamp posts to be posted next to number 53.

The issues do not always stop at parking. The Territorial often has a slightly different interpretation translating land ownership boundaries to HM Land Registry. Usually it would amount to 3cm on your land, which results in court cases running into tens of thousands of pounds, where the net land value in question amounts to £350.

You would of course ask why the Territorial does not log onto Land Auction websites where there is an abundance of strips of useless undeveloped land left over by developers or under flyovers with prices starting at £500.

The answer is the same reason why superpower empires and sphere of influences are geographically close to defend.

If the Territorial bought random land across the country, their paranoia levels would go through the roof.

Which leads to the next case study...

Case Study 7 – The Absentee

I quite like the Absentee neighbour. It is usually associated with empty lets, for sale properties or derelicts. The latter does have issues for devaluing your property, although the upside is that you have peace and quiet.

The property portfolio has been a reliable means of investing your money. There was the recession of 1990 which led to property values falling, and they threaten to fall again in the 2020s post COVID-19 years. However, people have made seriously large profits in property.

The curveball is land value. You may scroll through Rightmove advertising auction sites selling useless strips of land. Prices are low and for £1200 you could be the proud owner of a random grass verge in Accrington.

The question is what do you do with the random segment of land?

Well the result is that every so often the owner arrives and stands next to it for 13 minutes, initially on a weekly basis. There is an additional sense of pride as they think they are in the same upper-class social category as the country landowner, even if the reality is that they live in a semi in Runcorn.

Then the frequency drops to every two weeks, then monthly.

Then nothing happens. The owner appears the following year for 5 minutes then disappears again.

If the owner has a portfolio of a random selection of land, a planning application may appear for what is legally described as a one dwelling property, with their imaginative solution to the housing crisis being a pre-fab studio house measuring 12 foot by 7 foot 6 inches. Unsurprisingly, it is rejected by the council and you breathe a sigh of relief until an ominous looking sign appears reading TRESPASSERS WILL BE PROSECUTED.

The tension in the air is suspended, as are any plans to develop the micro space. Just like a soap opera, there is never an ending, just a continuation...

Case Study 8 – The Fortress

There are times when neighbourly relations are so bad that it can lead to taking it to the vets and shooting it.

Most houses have a defined boundary. The boundary is an indication to how excellent neighbourly relations are.

If relations are truly excellent, it will be a strip of concrete laid by the developer back in 1967. These are actually quite rare, and at the rate we are going, they will achieve Grade 2 listed status.

If you have good relations and wish to clearly identify your land, a 4ft fence may suffice. White planking in friendly neighbour boundaries, solid timber in average cases.

Where relations start become challenging, the boundaries increase to 6ft in height. If there is a relationship being maintained, the posts will be wooden. However, in cases where relations are – shall we say – at a point where less is more, the posts are concrete. This allows for creosoting to take place, where the panel can lifted out and you can keep out of your neighbour's way.

However, when neighbour relations are past the point of no return, the boundary needs to reflect the most suitable way to avoid any form of contact whatsoever. And so, we introduce the Fortress.

Hence, whenever you see a property with leylandii conifers, you can absolutely be assured the neighbours have fallen out.

If the property is completely surrounded by leylandiis, we can assume that the occupier is either a hermit or just cannot stand anyone in the neighbourhood.

If you are lucky, the leylandiis will be light green and yellow. However, the Fortress is often the ubiquitous dark green.

The end result is no light. Unless you like your garden to resemble a conifer plantation, which is favoured by investors, it manages to kill off any other plant species as well.

The Fortress is often favoured by the Legal profession for the thousands and thousands of pounds it generates for the profession.

Unfortunately, this is one of those cases where you really could do with the services of the Grudge, who could magic up some poison to kill off and miraculously fell the offending trees without being caught. However, you can expect a hefty prison sentence and a substantial fine for cutting 1cm off the branch.

Meanwhile, the burglar who has broken into your house under the cover of the offending conifer receives £100 compensation from the judiciary for the distress caused by the case being held up in Court by 20 minutes.

SHANK HIRE
LEZ COMPLAANT (HONEST)
EXECUTIVE
Travel
-STAG & HEN
-FOOTBALL PUNCH UPS
-PROM NIGHT
-FREE SICK BAG
-FRIENDLY SERVICE
-WILL GET YOU THERE AND AT LEAST HALF WAY BACK
Classic
AUTOFORNIA
KNAC7T
CLICK.....
TRR-TRR-TRR
RRR RRR RAARREV
REV
RRVVV

Case Study 9 – Bringing Your Work Home

Home working is becoming increasing popular these days. All you have to do is bring your laptop home and plug in. You are instantly connected to all your favourite colleagues and varied and interesting workload.

Your commute is straight to your desk. You do not have to endure the commute and personalities along the way – to be profiled in a future volume about travel.

Business benefits too. No more offices you have to heat and pay electric bills and business rates for.

There is the issue of bringing your work home and living the job.

Particularly if it means not storing it on a laptop or cloud.

Bringing your work home can often mean breezeblock appearing in next doors garden. Or drainpipes. Or windows. Piles of soil and asphalt appear as well.

If your interest involves the study of commercial vehicles, you are treated to a wide range of vehicles which will suddenly appear. Not quite classics – but in 25 years' time you will view the pristine examples at rallies and think back to the nostalgic times when they were on the road.

But in the here and how, a Luton Van will first appear. Then a florescent yellow lorry will be parked up on the road. The neighbours all park their cars outside so it then disappears.

You find your neighbour holds a PSV licence when a coach appears, proclaiming it is there to transport executives. Except it looks more suitable for a fax machine sales executive. Particularly when presented in the same condition as a 17-year-old fridge you come across in a layby. The misted double-glazed windows and condensation drenched curtains are excellent for privacy, but the semi bald tyre does not demonstrate confidence.

Bringing your work home is an excellent ethos to the modern workplace. Just watch out that the delivery driver does not leave you with 20 oil drums in your front garden by mistake.

COUNTRY LANES
WASTE COLLECTION SERVICE
COUNCIL (DIS)APPROVED

Case Study 10 – Walkies

There is nothing in the world which makes family life like a beloved pet. On the gloomiest day, they bring a ray of sunshine to your life. And if you are lucky enough to live next door to a pet owner, it can be a great way to get to know people.

Some neighbours have a very open-minded approach on how to look after their pets. This means that the pooch often wanders into your garden with a very unpleasant result, which you end up treading into your house.

Indeed, it has a knack of never leaving the footwear, and it often occurs when you are wearing designer footwear with deep tread or white trainers.

Sometimes the most particular owners train their beloved pet so it does not foul their garden but makes a bee line for yours.

Then you have the temperament of the dog which, in some cases, threatens to attack, but not as viciously as its owner.

You can console yourself that at least the dog will not be able to object to everything you do, which moves us onto the next profile.

CUSTOMER SPECIFICATION
- BRAIN OUT OF GEAR
- 0- CREDIT CARD - 2 SECONDS
- 12 POINTS ON DRIVING LICENCE
- REQUIRES IMPRESSIVE CAR TO SIT ON DRIVEWAY
RIPOFF MOTORS
AUTHORISED MAIN STEALER
GET OUT OF MY WAY
SHIFT IT
CAR SPECIFICATION
- 10 SPEED GEARBOX
- 0-60 MPH - 2 SECONDS
- 5MPG URBAN
- 5·2 MPG AVERAGE
- 6.1 MPG INTERURBAN
- PRIVACY GLASS
- ULTRA CLAUSTROPHOBIC INTERIOR
- PRIVACY GLASS
- COMPREHENSIVE ELECTRICS EXCLUDED FROM GUARANTEE
- INSTANT ACCESS TO SOCIAL MEDIA AND NEWS CHANNELS OPPOSITE TO YOUR POLITICAL VIEWPOINT
- FREE 18p TIN OF BEANS INTRODUCTORY OFFER TO YOUR NEW ECONOMY DIET
- 2000 MILES PER YEAR DISTANCE LIMIT
RIPOFF MOTORS SALES MANAGER SPECIAL
FINANCE
£8000-00 DEPOSIT
£0000-07 DEALER CONTRIBUTION
£983-00 PER MONTH OVER 120 MONTHS
£13275 BALLOON PAYMENT
APR 250%

Case Study 11 – Car Status Arms Race

Throughout civilisation, there has been an arms race between empires to gain supremacy. The end result has ended in a bloody battle, or in cases like the Cold War by treaty.

Some countries like to parade military hardware to emphasise their standing in the world. The leader inspects amazingly choregraphed troops marching alongside military machinery, which is not entirely suitable for the once a week shop at the supermarket.

And here we come to the Car Status Arms Race.

In these economically depressed times, there are arguments to have for a more equal society.

For those of us of a certain age, the equal society did not involve everyone driving Gene Hunt's Audi Quattro. It was more likely to have been a 10-year-old Vauxhall Chevette in pale yellow, with rusty edges. There were other fine cars like the Morris Marina, the Austin Allegro and the Ford Cortina. If you fancied a new car at half price, the Lada Riva was a popular choice. It boasted of having a 20-piece tool kit in the brochure.

Cars inevitably rusted and trips to the scrapyard were the order of the day. Cars were reconstructed with a mismatched collection of coloured front wings and doors which were meant to be resprayed, but no one ever got round to it.

Even in an equal society, some were more equal than others. Take for example the Austin Maestro. It was a popular choice in the 1980s. If you just about managed to scrape together enough money, you could afford the City model. If you were marginally better off, the City X version bought you a rear parcel shelf. You had colour coded bumpers in the more upmarket models.

Imagine a cul de sac with similar aged cars. One resident changes the car. Next door looks at their model and decides it is not good enough and changes theirs. Once the car has been bought, the owner suddenly decides they to want to park in the street. Then if you have not already noticed the new car, they go out and clean it. For three hours. The pattern is repeated and a few short months later the entire street has changed their cars.

In the more equal society, cars were bought with cash or bank loans.

Now the gloves are off.

PCPs are a way of allowing people access to a brand-new car. And in the car replacement arms race, it is no longer Maestro City X's being leased. Suddenly, the revolving car replacing cycle becomes more potent as expensive and aggressively styled premium brand cars appear on the drives, as the leases become even more expensive. The residents may be eating tins of beans and dry bread, but what's out of sight is out of mind...

Case Study 12 – The Random Car

There is one type of car owning neighbour which warrants a section all to itself. It is the Random Car – parked up in the street near you. Probably outside your house.

The UK is home to some 32.5 million cars. That is 32.5 million metal boxes on wheels, all of which need to be parked up at some point.

Most cars are kept in driveways or outside their owner's house. Or, in the case of the Territorial, outside everyone else's house.

Then, out of nowhere, a random car is parked up. If it is a prestige model, the Grudge will come out and leave a strategically parked dog turd next to the driver's door, smearing it on the handle for good measure. And if that doesn't get across the message, a curt message will appear on the windscreen threatening to vandalise the car if it is not moved. This usually works with the need for Phase 3, outlined in the note, rarely needing to be deployed.

The other type of random car is one which is extremely difficult to shift. It is usually owned by someone who has no connection to the area whatsoever, and just appears in the street one day. It usually falls into one of three categories:

1. A masterpiece of mediocrity. Often a mass-produced hatchback or estate. Colours are grey, plate green or brown metallic. Mileage is usually around 140k, which you can recall because you had to have a nosey through the window. The interior is death grey or soil brown. For security purposes, it may have a car lock with an extra-large keyhole, which any thief can remove by ramming a screwdriver in.
2. An unusual, specified variant of the above with additional extras like custard yellow wheels and piping on the bumper. The radio aerial is made of vandal proof rubber. The headlights are a tired lime green, ready for the continental touring holiday which never happened.
3. A very large motorhome in the similar style of the above, with the addition of a collection of lethal looking gas bottles stored inside.

Much as you are tempted to take up smoking and discard a still lit cigarette next to vehicle number 3, with the Grudge being nowhere in sight to make themselves useful, you report the vehicles as abandoned to the police.

Except it is not abandoned, as they have a full 11 months and 23 days MOT to run, and they have paid the same amount of road fund licence at a duty of £300, for a vehicle which will run no further.

You obsess over the DVLA website and discover the vehicle did pass the MOT, however, it had 17 advisories, including a tyre which is 0.005mm close to the legal limit. The owner did invest in having the driver's floor pan welded up in 2018 though.

After 12 months of wasting your life watching over the parked vehicle, it disappears in the middle of the night, leaving a large oil patch in its wake. You think you have got rid of it only to find it returns to sit outside your house just like a sinister stalker which has a Court Order to stay away.

Finally, it is MOT time and you seize the opportunity to leave your own car there. The space is yours and you have bagged it!

You are then in a predicament. You are paying off your PCP deal at £250 per month to have your (leased) car sat there doing nothing. Nonetheless, it is there in its rightful space and you have the satisfaction of knowing that the problem has gone away, and the offending vehicle has to park outside the Grudge's abode, or better still the Social.

Except your plans are thwarted when there is a knock at your door and the gas network need access to dig up outside your house to solve a gas leak. You agree to let them in to discuss the matter further because it is raining. They place the toolbox on your breadboard and walk across your white carpet with muddy boots, citing Health and Safety why they cannot be removed.

Once the work has been completed with an extended trench across your garden, the Random Car appears whilst you are not looking and is abandoned outside your house.

Several years later, you find an identical model destroyed on Top Gear and rant at the TV they should not be destroying the Nation's Motoring Heritage.

CRA 1 P

Case Study 13 – The Inquisitor

Many TV and movie detective shows have entertained us over the decades. The lead role usually comprises of a Detective Inspector and a sidekick. Think of Inspector Morse, The Sweeny, Scott and Bailey, Miss Marple and Inspector Wexford from The Ruth Rendall Mysteries.

All follow the clues relentlessly until the mystery is solved and the perpetrator is apprehended in a cliff hanging conclusion.

The Inquisitor in your neighbourhood makes it their business to know everybody else's business. When you move into your new home, they introduce themselves in an earnest and friendly way. They look up at you and their eyes pierce, and their face contorts like a gerbil looking through a jam jar.

The first questions start innocently enough. Where did you come from? What made you move here? Then we progress to "What job do you have?" If you are successful, the subject matter quickly moves on. If you find yourself in reduced circumstances, the subject hangs around like foul smelling drains and you find yourself dodging questions about where you previously worked.

Helpfully, the Inquisitor usually knows someone who works at your former workplace and is quietly satisfied to know you were placed on Improving Performance measures which you dipped in and out of during the last two and a half years of your former slowly dying career.

If you are downsizing, the Inquisitor will ask where you formerly lived. Once the conversation is over, they then research sold prices on your former street, then will know how you had to sell your previous home at a heavily discounted price by a speedy sales estate agent specialist. Afterwards, they then look to see it promptly re-listed as a rental or redevelopment project if you were unfortunate enough to have a dated kitchen or bathroom. You squirm because you forgot to remove the manky flannel and old towel when the bathroom photo was taken. Your new neighbour now has a permanent record of what your previous abode was like.

As the Inquisitor gets to know you, the questions become more personal. What is your marital status? What did you do throughout your career? If they are feeling bold, you may be asked how much your mortgage is. Of course, to be polite, they shamelessly add "if you don't mind me asking", to the end of the question. This backs you further into a corner, after all, is this an unreasonable question to ask, and do you really mind?

Did you have a difficult divorce? Their role of counsellor becomes invaluable as a resource to relieve poor mental health.

Helpfully, they will let you know all you need to know about your neighbours. In strictest terms, all you really need to know would be supplied by HM Land Registry, your local council's planning department and the Disclosure and Barring Service on a strictly need to know basis, in line with Data Protection legislation.

However, those agencies do not provide details about how the wife of number 5 is having an affair with the insurance broker on the High Street. Number 17 is approaching bankruptcy and are about to have the house repossessed.

Number 15 Grange Crescent has been recently diagnosed with severe haemorrhoids and receives an annual salary of £25,000 at the local council, having accrued 15 years' service. The pension benefits so far are £7000 pension per year and £6000 Lump Sum, should they wish to retire at 85. Co-incidentally, the Inquisitor also lives at Number 15 on your street with a similarly spelt street name.

The Inquisitor is one of your visible neighbours. They knock at your window instead of the front door when they call. If the door is unlocked, they invite themselves in. They appear on a pre-text and ask if they could borrow a spade or garden fork, even though their own stock exceeds a major DIY chain. Strangely, over the years, they manage to access every room in your house and find some spurious reason to access your front bedroom so they can have a view to see if their much-surveyed garage roof has a puddle on the roof.

As time moves on, the Inquisitor starts offering opinions. They start off with a sharp criticism of leaving a window open or a lawn mower left in the garden. Then we move onto how the marriage troubles at Number 19 should be resolved. After all, who needs a marriage counselling service when you have the Inquisitor at hand.

And thanks to Social Media, your affairs are not only shared within your street, they are also shared with 27 other people you will never meet, plus a further 67 former contacts who accidently clicked on "Unfriend" and changed their e-mail addresses and phone numbers simultaneously.

Then we turn to the Inquisitor themselves. Despite digging for other people's affairs like a dredger in Hull Docks, very little is offered about their lives. Their backgrounds range from the spectacularly dreary to being related to a Serial Killer currently locked in Strangeways.

MR A PEABODY
51 STREET AVE
SOLICITORS' LETTER
EMPLOYMENT TRIBUNAL
NHS
MR J NOBODY
TEST RESULTS
STDS

Case Study 14 – The Mad Driver

Thanks to social media, modern pressures and the rest of the neighbours profiled in this book, there is a need to express and take out the stress and frustrations of the day.

The usual course of action would be to enrol to a yoga class. Or if you really work for a bad organisation, a boxing gym would be a more suitable option. You can then pummel the punch bag until your heart's content.

However, this costs time and money and with a long hours working culture being the order of the day, this is a luxury which cannot be afforded.

So, this is where the Mad Driver comes in. There was a time when the Highway Code was diligently learnt, and every manoeuvre was carefully crafted.The test was joyfully passed at the fourth attempt. Once the test is passed, Mirror Signal Manoeuvre turns into Madly Stressed Maniac.

Thanks to careful research, we have a few examples we can profile: -

1) The Hatchback Horror

Usually leased on a PCP, the Hatchback Horror appears unassuming enough. The car is conifer green metallic and covers a low mileage and is handed back after four years. This does not get off to a good start when the car is parked on the wrong side of the road. When setting off, the car indicates right as it drifts across the road to the left. The driver then tailgates others like a possessed animal targeting its prey. Especially in fog and ice. The car starts off looking nice and new, but it doesn't take long for the bumpers to be scraped, wheels bashed against the pavement and roundabouts. It's favourite habitat is the concrete multi-storey car park sat very close to your car. It doesn't help when the owner has a poor sense of judgement and requires the turning circle of a HGV. At the end of the lease, the car is handed back to the dealer, the owner is caned for a heavy body shop bill, then resold as one careful owner.

2) The Historic Relic

Go to a vintage vehicle rally, and you will see plenty of pristine lovingly restored classic cars in tasteful colours and chrome fittings. In theory, all cars were once classed as old bangers reading for scrapping, however now you can purchase any car and it can be a classic. Any modern box has a cult status. The problem is when the car is "modified", tornado red and jade green metallic morphs into deep purple with lime green stripes. The wheels are then non-standard and are bright yellow with the suspension lowered to tarmac scraping levels. Stickers appear on the back some with abusive slogans. The Historic Relic then becomes a collection and start appearing around the street often parked outside your house. Parts become an issue and the owner thinks it prudent to obtain some examples for spares. Handily the garden comes into its own for storage. Unlike the Hatchback Horror, these are here to stay. When it comes to driving, the technique is to pull away at speed with the porous exhaust amplifying the noise. And that is all it can do, as it then breaks down and has to be pushed back home.

3) The Bull Barred Beast

The Bull Barred Beast can be applied to any type of vehicle; however, it usually features on a 4x4, truck or van. No mercy is shown to other motorists as the unique style of driving ensures dominance on the road. If you are in the overtaking lane, the owner will drive up threating to ram your vehicle. The Bull Barred Beast has other aftermarket features such as a blacked-out lights, windows and a blue light which lights up under the chassis. When the Bull Barred Beast is ready to park up, there is a unique process to stopping and locking up the vehicle. The vehicle slows, the door is opened, the engine is switched off, then the handbrake is applied.

4) The Two Wheeled Terror

Thanks to gridlock, there is a range of alternative means of two wheeled transport available. You can now relive

Speedway on country lanes on your motorbike, weave precariously between HGVs and buses and pavements on your bike, or shoot down pavements cutting down pedestrians on the way. The best thing is the government want you to cycle and has spent millions on cycle lanes. Except the cyclist does not want to use it and wants to pedal down the bus lane at 13mph and make everyone late for work.

Case Study 15 – The Social Leader

The Social Leader takes on a different profile to the rest of the neighbours. The Political Animal has a character which hinders them advancing in their cause.

The Social Leader is sickeningly positive and sugary sweet. Party invitations are handed out to neighbours for an event on a Sunday. In theory, this should be a nice way to spend the weekend, except nobody wants to be there and it ranks up the stress levels for Monday.

Events are usually BBQs, wine and nibbles or Tupperware parties. The latter involves a strict analysis of various plastic boxes, which makes reading the instructions to flat pack furniture appear fascinating by comparison.

You (and some of your neighbours) would rather go to the dentist for root canal surgery, so decline on that occasion. Unfortunately, excuses are not particularly well planned or co-ordinated, with the result being that seven households have an electrician coming round for an emergency, four houses have a gas leak and one household has subsidence.

The low attendance is rather embarrassing, so is made up of the Social Leader's social circle. On the night of the event, all neighbours have their blinds closed and are hidden out of sight. The guests arrive in a selection of weird looking cars driven by weirder looking occupants. The sales rep arrives in a people carrier and drags a suitcase which undoubtedly weighs the same as a concrete flag, leaving a trail across the grass verge. The evening wears on and you are relieved not to have attended as you watch an episode of Microwaves from Hell instead.

Invitations for other events drop through the door throughout the year. After attending a number of mind-numbingly boring events, you run out of appointments for gas engineers and electricians. You end up being self-evicted from your house, parked up near the nearest motorway service station just to get away.

The Social Leader takes charge of the local Round Table, Gala and Playscheme. Competition to lead is nil because nobody else can be bothered. After all, who wants to buy a semi dead plant from the Gala when you can dig up the same species near the local waste ground.

Unfortunately, there are several squabbles within various committees, which are less dignified than an episode of Question Time. The Social Leader has a meltdown as they balk at taking on too much work and everyone else not pulling their weight.

Like a crack cocaine user awaiting their next fix, the Social Leader is back again with a packed agenda, waiting for their three followers to join them for their next assignment to the nearest cul-de-sac to clean out the ginnel.

Case Study 16 – The Objector

There is a law in life that wherever you consider making a change to your life, there will always be someone who will object. The Objector will obsessively look at their neighbouring properties and will always find something which does not suit.

Take for example your submitted planning application to add a new porch to your home. Or a replacement garage. Before you know it, the Objector will be around to complain about your project. The door does not match. The windows are not to their style.

Sometimes they call around to your house claiming you have Japanese Knotweed in your garden, even though it isn't even there. Their eyes tighten and their face reddens as they insist it is there and point to a dandelion.

The Objector may have an agenda though, as the alleged knotweed is a cover for them to break your fence whilst demolishing their garden shed and demand it is on their border.

No matter what you plan, design and build, the Objector will work tirelessly to ensure that life is as difficult as possible. And when your builders arrive, who are signed up to the Considerate Contractors Code, the Objector will point out that one of the bricks left a scuff on the tarmac.

Unfortunately, for you, the Objector does not protest against large scale developments and vanishes without trace when the mega projects appear. As they micro-manage their lives and yours, every brick laid is analysed and criticised, and you sit in fear of the builders throwing in the towel and abandoning the project due to the incessant hassle.

So, when you next have the porch due to be built, book a month's holiday in Peru with no mobile phone signal, and ask your builders to place a board with a fake telephone number. By the time you return, the Objector will be onto their next project by micro analysing the colour of the tarmac the council has resurfaced the road.

Case Study 17 – The Watcher

Neighbourhood Watch Schemes have appeared over the country and have been a semi effective way to reduce crime. Would be burglars have cowed with fear as the Neighbourhood Watch stickers have appeared on porch windows, next to the UPVC zero rated security door. In theory, the Watcher is a real asset to the community and their services should be sought after.

Unfortunately, the Watcher is no use at all in cutting crime. In fact, no use at all, other than to watch the comings and goings of their neighbours. Their only use is to know and reprimand the leaflet distributor when the local classifieds is being dropped off late through the letterbox.

The Watcher seems to spend a lot of time at home and you wonder where they have made their money to be able to afford the upkeep of their neat and tidy home. Particularly as they never leave the house to clean the car or tend to the garden. The grass is a hybrid of seed species which never grows or needs cutting.

So, their activity is limited to sitting up like a meercat when neighbours arrive or leave their house. The newspaper flaps as their curiosity leads their intention.

Despite the availability of stickers on sale, instructing no junk mail is delivered through the letterbox, the Watcher has a habit of opening the door when junk mail is delivered and having a sharp word with the distributor.

I experienced this first-hand when I was delivering promotional leaflets for a business I was promoting. I delivered a leaflet to the house next door and the Watcher stood up. Hands were on hips. Lips pursed. I by passed the house. The Watcher was thwarted into a spasm of confusion. How could they not protest? What was the leaflet anyway? Their moment was snuffed out and it threw their mindset.

We may have to worry about climate change, pandemics and global social order, but the Watcher just focuses on the single issue of what is going on outside their house.

And when your car is broken into, you can be assured when you ask if they saw anything, the answer will be no.

Case Study 18 – The Challenger

The Challenger is a more general version of the Eager Listener. In modern HR, employees are encouraged to challenge each other in order to improve their performance. For those of us who just want to get through the day with as little hassle as possible, you are on the backfoot, and pray for another lockdown just to avoid all of this.

The Challenger is also one of those who ask multiple questions at the end of a training course when you want to leave for lunch, or you have a bus to catch, or wait for the next one an hour later. You sit tight and watch your evening be drastically reduced as they probe the trainer and put their points across.

If you work in customer services, you can be guaranteed that they will call five minutes before closing time with a formal complaint. And they will ask you for your name, your manager's name, the name of the director and the formal complaints department. Then they copy in their MP for good measure so you have to leave your employer to gain any chance of promotion.

The Challenger has excellent interpersonal skills. Or their job description states they have excellent interpersonal skills.

And as the Challenger has a home life; you will therefore be challenged. They place a water butt on your land to hide your bin. If you need to access your bin, you are then told you are unreasonable. A Christmas card is put through your letterbox asking you to move your car from outside your house.

Your garden slopes on their land because it is located on what is historically called a hill. However, that isn't good enough, because they demand you spend a five-figure sum levelling your garden and being the only house in the street who will do so.

They take a dislike to your car port installed since the house was built and will incessantly ask for it to be dismantled. Even though it is on your land and borders an unrelated neighbour's property.

The Challenger can sometimes have a classic hybrid personality combination of the Territorial, Social Leader, Political Animal and Grudge all rolled into one package.

Then they clog up the drains with nappies and cooking fat, and it's your responsibility to get the drains cleared.

Case Study 19 – The Liberty Taker

On the face of it, the Liberty Taker is one of the least offensive people you can come across.

This makes the issue all the more difficult as it creeps up on you unexpectedly.

It usually starts by parking outside your house. Then they have their driveway resurfaced and ask if they car park their car on your drive. Once the driveway is completed, their car stays on your drive. It finally returns to their house, except it periodically re-appears on your driveway.

Then you receive a polite request if they could store their bins on your land. It is just a hidden area and it looks better there than being in their garden. You feel obliged to agree but regret it afterwards as rubbish is stored on your land.

The liberties go further. The dog fouls your garden. The bonfires are lit behind your house, and so you are blamed by the local friends of Maybury Common Society. Your gravel path is dug up so they can have a new fence erected. Except the fence was yours, and what was a private 6ft barrier is replaced with a 4ft fence, which – annoyingly - means you see them all the more.

It cumulates when they nominate the Utility companies to route the pipes and cables across your front garden, so they do not have to have the disruption.

The phrase please don't ask as refusal often offends need not apply here.

Case Study 20 – Home Deliveries

Shopping used to be a pleasure. You drove to a car park and walked into a carefully designed outlet to buy your wares, also known as the retail experience. None of these outlets had useful facilities known as clocks because they hoped you would forget about time and spend more money. The punchy rock music would encourage you to spend even more money. The sales staff will helpfully steer you towards the stock that nobody wanted so as to avoid incurring penalties. Behind the shiny façade and your new friends is a stock room. Motivational notices are mounted with phrases like "DO NOT FAIL", "ONLY FAILURES FAIL", and "THIS WEEKS TARGETS ARE..." above the chewed biro and TV Quick magazine.

No more.

Thanks to the internet, high streets are boarded up and anyone can watch The Apprentice and subsequently call themselves a captain of industry by setting up a vendor's account online.

Your neighbours often shop on the internet. And they are usually out when the deliveries arrive. Strictly speaking, they should use a facility to purchase and collect their wares. This is known as a shop.

However, because they are forward thinking, they use the internet. And that means home deliveries.

At the start, they were delivered by professional companies using smart delivery vans. That meant they were delivered to the correct address – in theory.

However, thanks to the explosion in internet retail, there are a range of delivery organisations using low cost employment policies to ensure value for money.

The result is a race to deliver parcels as quickly as Santa on steroids. There is no Rudolph and a Sleigh. Just a 17-year-old small hatchback with three-wheel trims and a questionable MOT. Nor is Santa paid 15p per parcel delivered. With them being part of the prestige or being Self-Employed, and part of the incredibly cool sounding "Gig economy".

The parcels end up being delivered to the incorrect address. Yours.

The rap on the door knocker is so hard, or the doorbell is jammed in, that you feel like putting a notice up stating, "Please be gentle with me" or "Out of Order".

Notes are left through your door stating that the parcel your neighbour ordered is at the sorting office 50 miles away. You open the bin and discover another parcel.

You permanently live with the blinds closed so you are not seen.

You open the back door only to have a dog kennel flatpack fall on you which you never ordered.

And of course, it is expected you must take the parcels round as your neighbour cannot be bothered to collect them.

On the rare occasions that you go internet shopping, you can guarantee your parcel is posted to Ex-Prisoner Pete and Shoplifting Charlene, who will gladly sign for the goods with a totally unrecognisable squiggle.

Case Study 21 – The Security Junkie

It is estimated that 10.9 million offences were experienced by adults aged 16 years and over in the year ending September 2019. Vigilance is key to Crime Prevention and there are various measures which can be taken to reduce crime.

The Security Junkie cannot take the credit for the Neighbourhood Watch Scheme. This is credited to the Social Leader. Until the crime levels increase and everybody else is blamed.

The Security Junkie is a rather different type altogether. They are rarely seen and the only evidence that they exist is a collection of security measures which will put the fear into anyone with ill intentions.

The first high security measure that appears is a "Watch out, there's a thief about" sticker, next to the semi dead plant in the front porch window. If that does not scare away the would-be burglar, the faded primrose yellow Neighbourhood Watch sticker will.

Then a security lamp is fitted. The harsh beam pops on and off every time the cat prowls by. It is usually directed towards your bedroom window so you don't get any sleep.

The burglar alarm is set up with the flashing light at both the front and back of the house.

The mediocre beige hatchback with contrasting grey interior has a steering lock sticker mounted on the rear window next to the Visit Prilly's Caravan Park sticker, together with the main dealer, which closed ten years ago and is now a UPVC windows showroom.

The £495 caravan has a menacing looking wheel clamp. There is a single CCTV camera mounted above the car port which provides black/grey grainy footage, with all the accuracy of thick fog.

The 3ft front gate has a padlock attached, with a separate box attached for the mail.

All of which is a complete waste of time as the house contains goods which you could never shift on eBay as an honest trader, let alone to a dodgy contact down the pub.

There is a different type of Security Junkie which can be found in affluent areas. Behind the massive gates with the gold-plated Bull's heads at either side, there is CCTV located at every crevice, and the owner has six rottweilers threatening to rip anyone apart who dares look at the property.

This is also a waste of time as they head up the county criminal network. Any would be thief can be assured a new and fulfilling career serving alongside concrete filler, propping up under a newly constructed motorway.

Case Study 22 – Smokey

The word Smokey conjures up an image of the late great Burt Reynolds in a cowboy hat and a racing car.

But this is no Burt Reynolds tribute and there are no cars. Just smoke.

Despite most houses now having central heating and householders having access to recycling bins, there is technically no need to have a bonfire.

Technically, there is also no need for loud music or road rage either. But these things happen, and for whatever reason they must have the bonfire.

Timed for perfect blue summer days when you have the windows open and the washing on the line to dry, Smokey lights the fire without notice.

It starts with a thin wisp of light smoke. Then the fire is pummelled so it produces a thick plume of white smoke. So not only is your washing ruined, your house and soft furnishings stink of heavy smoke. To add insult to injury, Smokey will puff a tax-free cigarette whilst stoking the fire.

With the frequency of the fires in the summer days, you actually wonder what Smokey finds to burn. You look at the garden and see it does not generate too much waste and it is not autumn when wet leaves need to be raked up and burnt.

However, there is always a steady stream of papers which generate thick smoke, redundant furniture, plastic bottles, and if you are really unlucky, old drums of petrol.

Health and Safety legislation does not bother Smokey either. In the second role as community leader, the role of Bonfire Night co-ordinator was taken on. The fire is sited next to the local petrol station, car lot, camping gas store outlet and the UPVC storage yard. You can re-live old episodes of London's Burning in modern day reality.

Chapter 23 – Gardener's World

Neighbourhood gardens come in all sizes and designs, with a range of DIY chains and Garden Centres providing inspiration to make the best of your very own recreation area. Gardens tend to be categorised by the following:

1 Stately home inspired masterpiece with a beautiful range of shrubs, flowers and plants.
2 A paved and flagged development with feature plants planted around.
3 A green lawn with two leylandii conifers and a line of six widely spaced £2.99 bedding plants lining the front border.
4 A flagged garden comprising of paving slabs laid in 1976 and the £2.99 bedding plants.
5 A brick block parking area.
6 A bodged cowboy job brick concrete parking area with dried oil patches draining water on your land.
7 A rough lawn with a car or other vehicle parked on it, complete with tyre tracks gouged out of the grass (and your grass verge).
8 A display of washing lines displaying clothing of certain brands and colours, some with offensive and/or inappropriate slogans.

As neighbours come and go, gardens do evolve, and the pattern is for 1 to be replaced with 5 or 6.

If you live in a property which does not have a garden nor a courtyard or balcony, all the above can still apply but on a miniaturised version. Just replace the word car with wheelie bin.

Chapter 24 - Drill Baby Drill

A typical household will possess a range of furniture, a limited number of shelves and a handful of pictures per room.

In theory, to drill a hole to mount a picture, the timescale will be three seconds.

To drill a hole to fit furniture together, we can allow for six seconds.

To mount some shelves, lets allow for eight seconds per hole.

The drill is an amazingly efficient tool which allows for complex DIY to be achieved with ease.

It is also one of the most borrowed tools. The Inquisitor (profiled earlier) has quite a collection from several different households, as a pre-text for a more in-depth interrogation.

However, the Driller has a rather different agenda in mind. Drilling takes place every weekend and for hours at a time. It is used so frequently you wonder if there is anything left in the house to drill into. The house must resemble the appearance of Swiss cheese. There is no evidence of commercial activity, which could account for the frequency of use.

The drilling takes place when you are in the room adjacent to theirs. If you are in the bedroom, they will be in their bedroom. RRRRRRRRRRRRRRR.

Nip to the bathroom...RRRRRRRRRRRRRRRRRRR RRRRRR.

Working in the study to work on that complex spreadsheet. Your calculation takes place (B666RR:/?@ Z555555...interrupted by a RRRR. RRRRRRR you pick up where you left on only t...RRRRRRRRRRRRR RRRRRRR.

On Monday morning, you report that the sales figures for drainpipes has decreased dramatically in Cuba, when, in fact, you are reminded you work for a fashion retailer and were assigned to report on monthly sales trends in East Anglia.

Case Study 25 – Music? Maestro!

If you are famous, you may have your life story sold to the press. Or part of your life story. Or it could be a piece of complete fiction, however, because it was told by "a source", it is presumed to be true.

Motives arise by the green-eyed monster called jealousy.

Or, if you are a musician, they may have resented your practice sessions.

In theory, if you are excellent, this should not be an issue at all. Free tickets to see your favourite band? You would snap them up.

However, not all musicians are talented, and some are distinctly dreadful.

Spare time can induce boredom and as such hobbies are born. If you are a statistician and have no art skills whatsoever, you can take yourself to an art class and be asked to draw a dark green semi-dead plant. Your local golf club is desperate for new members, that is until you start to whack chunks out of the golf course due to your incompetence. Or you could start to destroy your house by taking up DIY. Nobody will notice the drainpipe that leads from your bathroom and down the staircase.

However, music is a different case altogether. Music is, in theory, a delight. However, your neighbours attempt to play an instrument is just noise. Drums are bashed. Guitars are thrashed on full volume. Violins are strangled. Pianos are clunked.

If you are lucky, your musical wannabee may be able to spew out three consecutive notes or be able to play one tune badly. And practice. And practice. Until you hear Tubular Bells bashed out on the piano several times in a row.

Worse, is the karaoke machine. Great hits over the decades systematically destroyed in seconds as Elvis Presley hits are groaned out. Pavarotti shrieked out. Right Said Fred's "I'm too sexy" belched out. Usually, this is suffered at the local pub, but now you have the karaoke machine available via the online catalogue for all of us to suffer.

You decide it is a good time to put the tumble dryer on.

Chapter 26 – The Refuse Collector

Plastic pollution, landfill and emissions burning rubbish are major environmental concerns. Today's consumer driven society, where tonnes of waste are generated by the millions, has contributed towards this major catastrophe. Fast fashion condemns clothing to waste, after being worn a couple of times. Electric cars are being built without the ability to recycle batteries.

Fortunately, there are forward thinking, environmentally aware citizens within our midst. And here is one such example.

The Refuse Collector does not work for the council. It is an example of an ultimate zero waste household. Quite simply, nothing is thrown away. Broken vacuum cleaners are retained just in case they can be repaired or harvest useful parts. Refuse is stored in sacks. Not just in kitchens, but up the staircase. Up against the walls so the walls turn to black mould; the smell is distinctly unpleasant. However, the Refuse Collector is unaffected.

The Refuse Collector does not contribute to chemical pollution, so bleach and other cleaning products are not used to clean, and the house remains unpainted. Ever cost conscious, money is saved, and builds up under the heavily stained mattress.

There may be pets, and once again, fouling the pavement does not occur as it all takes place on the kitchen floor. And the lounge carpet. As well as the hall stairs and landing.

The Refuse Collector is always popular at the office party as they can supply a range of charity raffle prizes. The lucky winner is delighted with prizes such as a used car glass fibre kit dating back to 1981, a recently decommissioned toaster, or a headless He Man figure for the serious collector.

The local Environmental Health department does have the occasional issue, however, after a good tidy up, the collecting starts again.

Case Study 27 – Water, Water Everywhere

Cleanliness is often referred to as godliness. After all, when you check into a hotel you expect nothing else.

Many residents are house proud, and DIY is a major passion for many. The results speak for themselves, with pristine houses which are a real asset to the neighbourhood. This really is something to be commended – nearly.

In the age of water shortages, it is often a requirement for water to be used sparingly.

This does not affect the ultra-cleaner though. High pressure jet washers are used for the car, sprinklers used for hours on the garden, and the drive needs a clean every two days. By a jet wash. And not for 30 seconds. Usually for a full hour.

And don't forget the drainpipes. White for practicality. And they have added UPVC cladding in place of tiles. So, this means the whole house must be washed and wiped down.

Life is well ordered, that is until the local Water Authority has to turn off the water supply for maintenance. Then it is switched on again with brown sedimented water. And that does not end well...

Case Study 28 – The Christmas Horror

Christmas is a joyous time of year. It celebrates the birth of Jesus and is the bedrock of Christianity.

It is celebrated in Churches and schools, and has the added advantage of upturning the nations GDP. Unwanted gifts including brown socks, aftershave which smells like air freshener, and this book you are now reading, are hastily despatched to the nearest charity shop in the New Year, pending the next trip to landfill.

Your neighbour's houses are accordingly decorated for Christmas. The Social Leader is first to put up the Christmas decorations on 15th October, only to be ripped down on 20th December. The Downturner does not bother this year as per the last five years. The Grudge prepares to nail a dead animal on the front door which belongs to the Territorial. The Inquisitor places an impressive selection of Christmas cards, hoping nobody reads them because they are blank.

There is one property in the street dripping with more lights than Blackpool Illuminations. It even upstages the local High Street. Which is rather embarrassing for the cash strapped Parish Council. The Disclosure and Barring Service checked Father Christmas turns up in a

Hyundai Getz to switch on the tired Christmas lights dating back to 1984. The Ex-Regional TV Presenter booked in could not make it due to be being detained because of drink driving the previous night. At least the semi dead Leylandii Christmas tree cannot be seen in the darkness or November murk.

To add to the Christmas toxic mix, all of the neighbours happen to have relatives who display equally dysfunctional behaviours.

To get away from it all, the Security Junkie jets off to Malaga, leaving every light switched on including floodlights, with the burglar alarm sounding every 21 minutes so nobody can sleep over Christmas.

Case Study 29 – The Property Boomer (Extensions, Digging Underground)

Since the turn of the century, the country has undergone a property boom. Thanks to increased demand through being able to obtain a mortgage five times your salary and buy to let, house prices have soared. This is deemed as a "good thing", as it is deemed to be a result of a successful economy. Papers boasted headlines state that Britain is booming and one of the arguments used to stay in the EU is that if we left, house prices would stop rising.

There is the rather small matter of people not being able to buy or rent houses, but this need not concern us as we analyse the fizz and the froth of the property boom.

This opened up countless opportunities to print money, as developers have moved into residential areas to renovate dilapidated properties. Often, this just means a trip to the wholesalers to install a basic trade kitchen and bathroom, complimented by plaster and paint. Such niceties like the roof, disinfestation, damp and electrics, tend to be overlooked in the hope the purchaser opts for a budget survey. The budget survey involves the surveyor pulling up, seeing whether the house is intact and driving off. After all, who bothers looking at a roof when that budget exclusive to trade bathroom suite has the wow factor.

If you are lucky, it will be a hit and run developer. A tight budget often means a tight timetable, and it really will be case of minimal effect for maximum return.

If you are unlucky, a planning application will be submitted. To submit a planning application means a serious amount of money is going to be invested and that means maximum profit.

Extensions and redevelopments become interesting to the student of architecture. The lines of the extension bulge off the side of a house and offer no continuity of the original design. Think of a really bad facelift. Or of an aging car design when the front and rear lights were designed by a different designer. Or perhaps go the whole hog, where a bus lost its roof under a bridge and the company despatched it to a different body manufacture for a new roof. The end result was, to put it mildly, dysfunctional.

The property could be a bungalow with a nice garden, with a proposal to transform it into 15 flats with underground car park. Basements of terraced properties are gouged out with worrying amounts of rock and soil transported away in skip after skip. The end product being an underground swimming pool with a sprinkler system which is just about to develop into your new major damp problem.

Interesting features appear. A balcony on the roof, so your privacy is lost forever. A revolving water fountain which sprays water in your garden. A shower appears in the loft. A toilet appears in the coal shed which is jammed against the wall so the user cannot turn around. Wall to wall tarmac surrounds the development, so your garden ends up resembling marshland. After all, you need not worry about ever having to water your garden again during a drought.

Surely conservation areas would offer protection to the quality of the design? Don't be so sure, as it depends what the policy is. Old buildings can be demolished and replaced with a large block of flats, complete with mock stone cladding in a low cost, feeble effort to match the surroundings.

Then we have the construction of the building itself. Many developers have a strict code of conduct. Builders manage to drive HGVs and diggers with the same discretion and disturbance as a cyclist.

Not your new neighbour. They manage to hire contractors who have a more relaxed interpretation of the Considerate Contractors code. Breezeblock is promptly delivered upon your grass verge. The request to allow you access to your property is interpreted as "Please block my drive and place your cement mixer next to my car". After a week of tolerating the cement mixer splattering your car with concrete and sandblasting the stonework whilst you have your washing out, you decide to take action. Your polite request that they could perhaps kindly move the equipment is met with protest. Huffing and puffing! After all, where else can they put their gear? Of course, you could offer your services to act as Logistics Project Manager, however, that would mean invoicing your developer neighbour for £11345 plus VAT, adding to their overall costs.

Once the masterpiece is completed, the contractors disappear to deliver havoc upon their next victim, and the property stands impressively like a brand-new nuclear power station style block of flats upon what was once a tired brick- built bungalow. The tired flagging and RSPB sticker in the front porch are consigned to history. And now comes the time to sell the masterpiece.

Estate Agents arrive to value the development. They often appear in premium branded cars. Some may have their own name on the side. They range from the sharply dressed up and to the slightly dishevelled who only stay in business because they are cheap.

Clipboards are thrust around, and 4K spec photos are taken. The 'For Sale' board appears, but you await the details to appear on the website. There is a delay – to build up the anticipation.

Then, after a few months' peace, your new neighbours arrive. And you have some or all of the same problems all over again.

Case Study 30 – Unfinished Business

With the rise of daytime TV property programmes, the retired, students, sick, home workers and unemployed, have a wide range of property programmes to be entertained with. Punctured with TV adverts advertising conservatories, Equity Release and super quick loans at 125% APR, it is so easy to get caught up in the feel-good factor of property profits.

Semi-dead houses are brought to life. Musty kitchens and bathrooms that have a spiral staircase in the centre of the lounge are transformed into a modern, contemporary home in a two-minute clip. The presenter and owners' guffaw as they discuss how they made a £75k profit.

The previous owner may not enjoy their home appearing on National Television, assuming they are still alive.

So, you may think you are reading another Property Boomer chapter – well, not quite.

With the property renovation industry being popular, it means anyone can join in. Imagine, you buy a car to renovate for £40. Then you find out it is rotten underneath, requires new sills, suspension, engine, gearbox, doors and tailgate, and before you know it, you need to spend £5000 to return it to the road.

Property is just like that, except you just add a few 0s at the end of the figure.

But here is the trap. Unless it is an absolute classic, the car is despatched for scrap, and the would-be project owner can pass it off as an abandoned car.

The house on the other hand can go up in value. Assuming it is in an area where prices do go up. And to compound the problem, the owner is cash strapped, debt averse, and perpetually under the threat of unemployment.

So, to manage the project, the finances are super cautious. The damp proof course is completed in Year 1. The electrics in Year 2. The owner goes without a TV and regards a toaster as a luxury. After five years, an extension is started, only to be completed in Year 17.

The list becomes longer and the house takes on an appearance resembling an episode of Auf Wiedershen Pet. Contractors fail to turn up, delaying progress even further.

The owner's mortgage liability drops to the value equating to a ten-year-old city car, then finally the masterpiece is finished.

Then the owner becomes tempted with another bargain, decides to sell up, and the cycle happens all over again.

Case Study 31 – Neighbours Up and Down and All Around. The Curse of Flats

An apartment can often be a desirable place to live. Stunning views. Nice people. Secure accommodation. And with a national housing shortage, they are becoming more popular than ever, especially as bungalows are demolished with eight flats being built in their place.

It is the other place where all the neighbour personalities profiled together are compressed together in one location, where views can be expressed and actioned.

Like subletting, flats have two additional personalities who reside in them:

1) The furniture mover and scraper.
2) The boot stomper.

A lounge would typically comprise of a three-piece suite, a TV and a cabinet. The dining room would host a table and chairs. The bedroom would have a wardrobe (sometimes fitted) and a bed. So far so good.

The furniture may be moved to clean or re-arranged once every couple of years.

However, the Mover and Scraper has a knack of moving furniture or other large objects every day. The process takes a full hour or two, just at the point when you settle down to watch another unmissable episode of Celebrity Abattoir Worker followed by Question Time.

There is a change of mind where the sideboard needs to be. A spontaneous decision is made to move it at 2.00am in the morning.

The Boot Stomper is usually seen with normal footwear such as suede shoes or trainers. For some reason, there is a need to wear extra clunky boots inside the flat. This does add protection against laminate flooring and provides a clear indication as to how the boots are hitting the floor, so the user is absolutely clear where they are putting their feet.

If you find this a real issue, you can knock at the door to speak to the resident. However, why bother when given how poorly constructed some modern flats are, you can access next door like the drunk partygoer who stumbled and burst through the plasterboard to join their neighbours watching TV.

UNIT3B
STACCCKO
INDUSTRIAL
ESTATE
FOR HIGH QUALITY CRATES
THINK STACKHI
- PLASTIC-BOXY
- COLOURED LIDS
- INSPIRATIONAL
- ALSO AVAILABLE TO BE SET
IN BRUSHED CONCRETE
DON'T
MESS WITH
ME....

Case Study 32 – The Curse of Commercial

In the 1930s, Britain had a major housebuilding development where semi-detached properties were built along main roads. Then the Green Belt was created, and restrictions were placed where developments could be planned out.

The legacy was properties which enjoyed a pleasant view across the green and pleasant land. Traffic was light and the air was fresh.

The decades moved on and the countryside became urbanised. New housing developments were built. If you were lucky, they merged within or enhanced the area. If you were unlucky, your pleasant semi-detached would have a retail park or industrial estate lumped next door.

The planning application is made, and the notice appears on a lamppost on the next street. The notice mysteriously vanishes. The construction traffic appears and your next summer is ruined by the continuous clanking and rumbling of construction works. Helpfully, a flyover is constructed next to your house relieving it of the prevailing wind. A multi directional traffic lighting system is located at the end of your drive which allows for traffic to build up and is designed so the exit from your driveway takes just 37 minutes. The upside is that there is no need to invest in Christmas lights. You complain about lorries driving over your verge, so ugly concrete domes appear.

Your view from your garden is transformed by low rise clad cubes with brash logos. Some are household names whilst others you have never heard of. Fast food aroma drifts across your garden through the daytime and there is a pungent smell of diesel in the air. Thankfully, there is a bus service as part of the developers' green travel agenda. The bus is timetabled every two and a half hours and is used by 3 people a day and is run by a one vehicle independent bus company. The vehicle comes in dealer stock white, ready to be swiftly returned to the leasing company once the contract is pulled.

You do have the advantage of not having to pay out for security lighting as the EU GPP Criteria for Street Lighting & Traffic Signals standard lampposts are newly installed in your neighbourhood to full motorway standard.

Your culinary needs are taken care of with the services of the industrial estate sandwich van. If your property is located at the start of the one-way system, you do have first choice of a wide selection of mouth-watering sandwiches. The advantage is reduced should your property be located at the exit point; however, the remaining cress and prawn sandwiches will ensure maintenance of a healthy diet.

However, the noise, diesel pollution and view grinds you down. Although you cannot have a personality clash with Unit 4 Lane One Industrial Plc in the same way as someone living in a house, it is less than ideal. You place your house on the market and the Estate Agent markets it as ideal for motorway links and shopping.

F&#K OFF!
BUS STOP
FIGHTING UNFAIRLY CHANTING & KICKING

Case Study 33 – The Nuclear Family from Hell

We have to leave the best until last. The much-vaunted Nuclear Family from Hell. The TV shows which bring real lives to our sofas. Previously, actors, script writers and production crews were employed to entertain us.

No more.

The modern TV schedule comprises of 24/7 news, misery on Albert Square, and reality TV. This usually comprises of high viz vests emptying bins or larger than life personalities in their home surroundings, otherwise known as Neighbours from Hell.

The Nuclear Family from Hell is something rather special. It comprises of some or all of the characteristic behaviours in this book. Unlike the soon-to-be-swatted fly on the wall documentary, we take a deeper analysis using three profiles.

1. The Nuclear Kiloton Family

We start off with the low yield Family from Hell with the Kiloton Family. The parents are usually in employment and have successful careers or businesses.

As the parents work in excess of 70 hours per week, their offspring sometimes do not have the inclination to follow suit. And as such they test the boundaries.

Under normal circumstances, this would be known as "Terrible Twos". Toys are thrown, chocolate rubbed into the carpet, and Thomas the Tank Engine participates in an NCAP crash test with the skirting board.

During the childhood years, care and educational stimulation are provided by a nursery or nanny. Fun games are played, and creative artistic activities are initiated with paint and canvas.

The Kiloton Kids then take things a little further. As they grow up, it all starts off rather innocently with PVA glue and glitter spilt on your brick block drive. It is followed up by planks of wood pulled away from the fence. Stones are thrown at windows. Halloween is spent with trick or treaters demanding £10 and the car will be left alone. The local car detail franchise has an unexpected windfall in car bodywork restoration work.

The good news is that the Boarding School offers a respite for 38 weeks of the year. The Kiloton's are chauffeured across in their parents' premium brand 4x4. In theory, the Kiloton kids undergo a high-quality education as a springboard to the boardroom. Unfortunately, the Principle does not take kindly to crack cocaine poured into the sinks and toilets, as the outcome leads to flood damage. As such, a review occurs and the Kiloton's are either expelled or suspended depending upon the parent's income and social influence.

The Kiloton's then expand their social circle with an interesting mix of people. Parties are held in their parent's absence. High volume musical appreciation, pharmaceutical sampling, cumulating in their inner Lawrence Llewelyn-Bowen restyling the interior of the property in an avant guarde abstract layout.

As soon as the Kiloton's hit 17, they have a crash course in driving and sign up to a brand-new premium brand sporty hot hatch. However, six months later, the NCAP crash test is repeated using a skip after six months motoring. With the £9,500 insurance premium paid, they are back on the road again.

University beckons and the Kiloton's are exported to a Russell Group University City. Your problem is moved over to become the Michelin Starred restaurant's challenge as the Dining Club hits the town. Criminal charges are escaped as one of the party's influential parent's pay to refurbish the premises. Imaginative Student Initiation Rituals follow and are later described in Court, or in a biography profiled by the *Mail on Sunday*.

The University experience usually has one of two outcomes. If there is a family business, it results in expulsion, followed by an immediate appointment to the Board of the family firm.

The second outcome involves purchasing a First-Class honours degree transcript to use in exams, followed by a placement to a Blue-Chip plc via family influence. For many, placements usually involve making the tea, buying the sandwiches, unshredding the photocopier and cleaning the toilets.

The Kiloton has a happier experience. High quality mentoring is willingly provided by staff keen to retain their employment. There is a notable absence of challenges. The appointment is made at the plc, and a personality transformation suddenly occurs. Staff are no longer allowed to talk, and the workforce is regularly refreshed via a bi-annual corporate restructure.

2. The Nuclear Megaton Family

We now move onto the medium yield Family from Hell with the Megaton Family. The parents may be in some form of employment which can comprise of either selling goods sourced at zero cost, or have a successful career in Corporate Britain at the local poultry farm. As the parents have a varying attitude to the work ethos and a relaxed approach to legalities, their offspring follow suit. They do not need to test the boundaries as there aren't any.

During the childhood years, care and educational stimulation is provided by the City Bus company in the form of a free Dayrider ticket. Fun games are played such as opening the rear emergency exits and engine covers. Creative artistic activities are initiated on the seat backs in the form of pen and ink, or carvings.

The Megaton kids develop on the theme of their childhood upbringing. As they grow up, it all starts off rather innocently with paint spilt on your drive. It is followed up by spraying graffiti on your house wall. Concrete blocks are thrown at windows. Halloween is spent with trick or treaters demanding £20 and the car and house being "promised" to be left alone. The local car glazing franchise has an unexpected windfall in car window replacement.

The good news is that the local school offers a respite for 38 weeks of the year. The school contract bus ferries the Megaton's, their classmates, and most of the bus seats to and from school. In theory, the Megaton kids undergo an education as a springboard to earning a living. Unfortunately, the Headteacher does not take kindly to a fire being started in the prefab classroom. As such, a review takes place. The Kiloton's are either expelled or sent to a specialist behaviour unit. The latter, depending upon if the parents are high on crack and their ability to communicate coherently after their last fix.

The Megaton's then expand their social circle with an interesting mix of people. Parties are held at their parent's house. The parents are present in body, but not mind. The party comprises of musical appreciation of a similar beat of music to the early hours. Every other word of the sophisticated conversation usually name checks a well-known designer fashion brand. Or at least something sounding like it. As the house is already set out in an avant guarde abstract layout, there is less of a need to consider their inner Lawrence Llewelyn-Bowen.

As soon as the Megaton's hit 14, they have a literal crash course in driving and appear in a range of "borrowed" vehicles. Many undergo a flame-resistant test in the nearby woods, but all fail miserably. NCAP crash tests are repeated using various street furniture. However, with no insurance premium to pay, they are back on the road again.

The University of Life beckons and the Megaton's carry on pretty much as before. The house is regularly upgraded with the latest entertainment equipment, which started out life in the homes of the other Case Studies in the book.

Just as the Kiloton's meet likeminded people in the University Hall of Residents, the Megaton's increase their social circle. The neighbouring properties become occupied with residents who have a similar outlook on life. There is the rather small matter that none of them get on with each other and are a toxic soup of the Case Studies profiled in this book.

The free cars and entertainment equipment on tap, do allow for social progression to take place. As the Megaton's do not work for a living, they are less worried about Corporate Restructures. However, with each resident maintaining a £99.99 per month Cazaksio Visionnaire 2100 mobile phone, it does take its toll on the needy family's finances.

However, this is relieved by a brief stay, from time to time, in a HM appointed Residential complex with free food. The downside is the judge decides upon the length of the stay rather than Booking.com.

3. The Tsar Bomb Family from Hell

We close the Case Studies with the ultra-devastation - The Tsar Bomb Family from Hell. Named after the largest nuclear device to be detonated, the Tsar's leave a waste ground of devastation in their wake.

The parents head an unbranded pharmaceutical franchise. As the parents accrue large amounts of tax-free income, their offspring follow suit without boundaries such as HRMC, the police and Customs and Excise.

"Terrible Twos" are quickly bypassed and their offspring mature very quickly.

During the childhood years, care and educational stimulation is provided by mixing with other children brought in from random parts of the country. Fun games such as pass the parcel are played, and happily the presents can be taken home to be distributed to needy people in their communities.

The Tsar Kids then take things a little further. As they grow up, it all starts off rather innocently with an interest in specific kitchen utensils. It is followed up by watching The Apprentice and a desire to set up a business. Buying and selling activities take place at the local park. Halloween is spent by trick or treaters demanding the deeds to your house or a cut in your salary, with the outcome being that you can expect to have a near normal life expectancy. The local car recovery firm has an unexpected windfall in collecting a torched-out wreck which once belonged to a customer with credit control issues.

The good news is the local school offers a respite for 38 weeks of the year. The Tsar's are chauffeured across in their parents' bullet proof premium brand 4x4. In theory, the Tsar's undergo a high-quality education as a springboard to employment. Unfortunately, the Headteacher, social services and the police, do not take kindly to a franchise being set up in the school. As such, a review is taken place and the Tsar's are either expelled, suspended or ignored, depending upon the parent's income and social influence.

The Tsar's then expand their social circle with an interesting mix of people. Parties are held in the parent's absence, which comprises of dull base sounding musical appreciation. This cumulates in their inner Lawrence Llewelyn-Bowen restyling the interior of the property in an avant guarde abstract layout. An ambulance arrives shortly afterwards.

As soon as the Tsar's hit 15, they have a crash course in driving and appear in a brand-new premium brand sporty hot hatch. The insurance premium is an optional extra, with a no fault guaranteed pay out by the other party.

University beckons and the Tsar's are exported to a University City. Your problem now becomes Thames Valley police's challenge as the franchise hits the town. Criminal charges are avoided as the parent's influence enables a third party to admit to the criminal charges instead.

The University experience usually has one outcome. A new franchise is set up, leading to an immediate appointment to the Board of the family firm.

The alternative outcome involves an exceptionally long stay at premises appointed by HM The Queen.

The Tsar has a happier experience with high quality mentoring and an absence of challenges. The appointment is made at the family franchise non-plc; however, the personality remains. Sub-franchise holders are not allowed to talk about their work, and the workforce is refreshed via mysterious disappearances.

The Departure

After all the swirl and micro-dramas over the years, it is time to move on. Rooms are full of crates with all your worldly possessions, and the van is parked outside.

All your annoying neighbours are about to vanish from your life, and you will never see them again. They will be just a memory, and technically all your problems will be solved.

I say technically, however, nature has a habit of replacing a void. There will be all of the same issues all over again in your new residence. Unexpected problems. Issues you could never make up. Dramas which technically should never arise. Neighbours moving in and out of your life like a revolving door.

Strangely enough, some actually come around to say goodbye. The serial killer look-a-like turns out to be normal, apart from the moment when there is a lingering look at your carving knives.

Of course, the move does not go smoothly because the Territorial has decided to park outside your house and leave to go to work when the removal van needs access. However, you do have the satisfaction of taping a "THANKS A LOT FOR PARKING HERE" notice on the windscreen. Particularly, as you have the satisfaction of then blaming the shyster moving in who kept trying to chip away at the agreed sold price and threatening to pull out of the sale the night before. After all, you were perfectly happy and had no issues regarding parking, didn't you?

Every so often you do drive past your old house. You track how it has changed. You note whose house is up for sale and wince as they received a better price, even though you sold yours in a recession. They could have a personality transplant when they move, but that will not happen.

The improvements to your old house are not to your taste, particularly when the house is re-rendered and painted in a lurid shade of browny-yellowy-orange with black windows and a bronze bull's head upon each gate post. The 10-year-old 4x4 bulks awkwardly in the drive, which was designed for a Hillman Imp when the house was built.

Acknowledgement and Thanks

Whilst writing this book, I would like to place on record my thanks to all of those who have provided the inspiration to make this happen.

Whatever misery they have inflicted on your neighbours, work colleagues and other road users, I can assure their endeavours have made it worthwhile, with the result being this fine publication you are now holding.

In todays' celebrity obsessed culture, where celebrity's car crash lives are played out in magazines located next to the supermarket checkout, we can have the privilege of having our own neighbours play out their lives for our own entertainment.

I salute you, but please keep my drive clear when parking your car. Especially not on the grass verge. And turn down the noise. Keep your garden tidy. Mind your own business. And no – I don't want to attend your party next Sunday evening.

www.ingramcontent.com/pod-product-compliance
Lightning Source LLC
LaVergne TN
LVHW051012080826
845145LV00009B/2579

* 9 7 8 1 8 3 9 7 5 4 3 6 4 *